SCIENCE, CHANCE
AND PROVIDENCE

UNIVERSITY OF
NEWCASTLE UPON TYNE
PUBLICATIONS

SCIENCE, CHANCE AND PROVIDENCE

The Riddell Memorial Lectures
Forty-sixth Series
delivered at the
University of Newcastle upon Tyne
on 15, 16, and 17 March 1977

BY

DONALD M. MacKAY

Research Professor of Communication
University of Keele

OXFORD UNIVERSITY PRESS
1978

Oxford University Press, Walton Street, Oxford OX2 6DP

OXFORD LONDON GLASGOW
NEW YORK TORONTO MELBOURNE WELLINGTON
KUALA LUMPUR SINGAPORE JAKARTA HONG KONG TOKYO
DELHI BOMBAY CALCUTTA MADRAS KARACHI
IBADAN NAIROBI DAR ES SALAAM CAPE TOWN

British Library Cataloguing in Publication Data

MacKay, Donald MacCrimmon
  Science, chance and providence. – (Riddell
  memorial lectures; 1977).
  1. Religion and science – 1946–
  I. Title II. Series
  215   BL240.2   77–30638
  ISBN 0–19–713915–9

*Printed in Great Britain
at the University Press, Oxford
by Vivian Ridler
Printer to the University*

'Sir,

'I perceive by what you intimate, that your friends Dr. W. and Mr. N. think it very strange, that I, whom they are pleased to look upon as a diligent cultivater of experimental philosophy, should be a concerned embracer of the Christian religion; though divers of its articles are so far from being objects of sense, that they are thought to be above the sphere of reason. But though I presume they may find many objects of the like wonder, among those with whom I am comprised by them, under the name of the new virtuosi; and among these, they may meet with divers persons more able than I, to ease them of their wonder; yet since they are pleased by singling me out, as it were to challenge me to do it, I shall endeavour to make them think it at least less strange, that a great esteem of experience, and a high veneration for religion, should be compatible in the same person.'

(From the introduction to
Robert Boyle, *The Christian Virtuoso*)

PREFACE

THE scientific enterprise to which our present civilization owes so much—for good or ill—developed in a context of biblical Christian faith. Its pioneers were happy to dedicate their new-found experimental methods 'to the greater glory of God'. The argument of these lectures is that this harmonious relationship between science and biblical theism is as natural and normal today as in an earlier age, and that conflict can arise only when key biblical emphases are distorted or forgotten.

I owe much to the insights and patience of friends and colleagues with whom I have discussed these things over the years. Chief among them is Professor R. Hooykaas, of Utrecht, whose book *Religion and the Rise of Modern Science* offers particularly apt historical illustrations of many points made here. I am also grateful to my friends Professor J. B. Lloyd and Dr. J. M. Forrester, and to my wife, for valued help in revising the text.

Finally it is a pleasure to record my thanks to the University of Newcastle upon Tyne for the invitation to give these lectures and for the gracious hospitality I enjoyed there. Professor David West, Pro-Vice-Chancellor, and my host Professor Roger Pain, are among many whose kindness I shall long remember.

D. M. MacKay

Keele, April 1977

CONTENTS

I. *A Scientist in God's World*

II. *The Mythology of Chance*

III. *What Room for Providence?*

I

A Scientist in God's World

1. *Fog*

IT would be hard to deny that science in our day, at least in the western world, is under something of a cloud. Recruitment to science courses in our universities is down: one reason, we are told, is that the young are disillusioned with science and anxious to turn their talents in directions offering a better hope for humanity. From a pedestal on which it shone as the brightest jewel in man's intellectual crown, science has fallen to be trodden under foot as a baneful influence, the polluter of the sweet simplicities of both the human spirit and the human environment.

For the Christian religion, at least in our country, it cannot be said that the sun shines much brighter. According to a previous Riddell Memorial Lecturer, Dr. Bryan Wilson,[1] 'All the evidence from our own times suggests that, at least in the western world, Christian faith is in serious decline. . . . Most modern men, for most of their time, in most of their activities, are very little touched— if they are touched at all—by any direct religious intimations.' Dr. Wilson attributes the decline to a sense of 'irreconcilable contradiction' between the suppositions of faith and the suppositions that underlie all other activities in which modern men engage in their everyday lives.

[1] Bryan Wilson, *Contemporary Transformations of Religion*, 45th Riddell Memorial Lectures Series, Oxford University Press, London, 1976, p. 6.

In some minds, indeed, science and the Christian religion are linked in their disgrace. If we listen to Arnold Toynbee,[2] for example, it is Christian monotheism, with its denial of the divinity of nature, that we should blame both for encouraging the rise of modern science and for 'removing the age-old restraint that was once placed on man's greed by his awe'. 'We have been taking unlimited liberties with nature because we have been thinking of her, in monotheistic terms, as unsacrosanct raw material.' The remedy, as Toynbee sees it, lies in reverting to a pantheistic view of the natural world—restoring the nature-worship that Christianity abolished; but the biologist Jacques Monod[3] waxes even more eloquent from an austerely anti-religious viewpoint that would have none of this. 'Armed with all the powers, enjoying all the riches they owe to science,' he declares, 'our societies are still trying to live by and to teach systems of values already blasted at the root by science itself.' According to Monod, the time has come to eradicate from the modern mind all remaining traces of what he likes to call 'animistic thinking'. 'Man at last knows that he is alone in the unfeeling immensity of the universe, out of which he emerged only by chance.'

Now although Dr. Wilson, in the lecture from which I have quoted, conveys an impression that he, too, came rather to bury Christianity than to praise it, I must confess that my intention on this occasion is precisely the opposite. I have indeed in my time felt the pull of views such as those I have cited, and can recognize the caricatures of biblical Christianity about which each is true as far as it goes. But as one who has been nourished for much of a happy lifetime in both science and the Christian faith, I am convinced

[2] Arnold J. Toynbee, 'The Genesis of Pollution', *Horizon*, **15**, no. 3, Summer 1973.   [3] Jacques Monod, *Chance and Necessity*, Collins, London, 1972.

that neither of them deserves the ill repute and neglect that have temporarily befallen them. If I am right, this is a serious matter. All over the world, men and women are turning to irrationalities of every kind in a desperate search for meaningful experience. If, as I believe, the Christian religion offers an alternative in which reason and faith can still find themselves harmoniously integrated, it is of more than academic importance to show that this is so.

I realize that more than one Riddell Memorial Lecturer before me has devoted himself to the reconciliation of science and religion. I think, for example, of my old friend Charles Coulson, who lectured in 1953 on 'Christianity in an Age of Science',[4] and wonder how I can add anything worth while to what such as he have said so well. Yet somehow the need for these clarifying operations seems perennial. There is today, it seems, a fog of confusion around the issue of science and faith quite as dense as that which enveloped the unfortunate Darwin a century ago. Even if wholesale fog dispersal is beyond our means in three short lectures, I hope it may not be too ambitious to try to clear the air around some of the main points at issue.

My plan will be the converse of the more traditional pattern of defensive apologetics. What I shall be arguing is not just that Christian belief is compatible with the methods and findings of science, but that from a theological standpoint the two belong together as naturally as root and fruit. So instead of starting with the scientific world picture as a given thing, solidly established on unchallengeable foundations, and then later asking what room is left for particular religious claims, it will serve our purpose better to ask first what it is that Christians believe our Creator has

[4] C. A. Coulson, *Christianity in an Age of Science*, 25th Riddell Memorial Lectures Series, Oxford University Press, London, 1953.

told us about the nature of our world: about its fundamental dependence (and our dependence) upon his creative power, and about the purpose for which he has brought us into being. Along this biblical-theistic path, if you will have the patience to follow me, I believe we shall then see the habit of mind we call 'scientific' emerging as something not incidental to Christian obedience, but rather naturally expressing it. I hope to show that any sense of 'irreconcilable contradiction' between the suppositions of Christian faith and those of science is in fact an illusion whose causes are understandable, but whose basis can be seen to be false whether or not one accepts the truth of biblical Christianity.

2. *Dynamic Stability*

'I believe in one God, Maker of heaven and earth.' So says the ancient creed of the Christian Church. The claim of biblical theism is that the world in which we find ourselves is not eternally self-sufficient; it has a Maker, on whom it depends not just for some initial impulse long ago, but for its daily continuance in existence now. This is strange language to our modern ears. The world we know seems very stable, reasonably law-abiding (in the non-human domain at least), and not at all obviously in need of any divine power to keep it going.

Over the past 200 years and more we have become accustomed to thinking of it in the image of a mechanism, intricate perhaps beyond the grasp of human understanding, but still something self-running and self-contained. Thinking in these terms, we might see some point in bringing in God as the original creator of the universe; but we might find it particularly hard to visualize any sense in which a universe, once created, could continue to depend on its creator for its existence.

Without pretending to fathom the mysterious depths of these biblical claims, I believe we can get some feeling for what they mean from the imagery of modern physics itself. Ask a physicist to describe what he finds as he probes deeper and deeper into the fine structure of our solid world, and he will tell you a story of an increasingly *dynamic* character. Instead of a frozen stillness, he discovers a buzz of activity that seems to intensify as the magnification increases. The molecules he pictures as the stuff of the chair you are sitting on—and of the body sitting in it—are all believed to be in violent motion, vibrating millions of times in a second, or even careering about in apparent disarray, with an energy depending on the temperature. Each of the atoms composing those molecules is thought of as a theatre of even more dramatic activity, at first likened by Niels Bohr to the whirling of tiny planets around a central sun, but nowadays pictured, if pictured at all, as the vibrations of a cloud whose shape and density determine the probability of various kinds of discrete events called light-emission, electron-absorption, and the like. According to modern physics, it is to such elementary *events*—myriads of them, continually recurring—that we owe all our experience of the solid world of objects. Even the fundamental particles postulated by theoretical physicists as the building bricks of our world are thought of as spending their time in snapping from one to another of a variety of different states, or even in continually exchanging identities.

For our present purpose it does not matter for how long physics is likely to go on using these particular images, to which we shall return in the next lecture. I have mentioned them now only to illustrate a key concept that I think may help us to grasp what the biblical writers mean when they say that the stable existence of our world depends on the creative activity of God. We can call it *dynamic stability*. In our everyday experience chairs, tables, rocks are typically stable objects. There they are. Nothing may seem to be happening to them, or in them, for most of their existence; yet the modern physicist is quite content to describe such stable objects of our experience as a concurrence of unimaginably complex and dramatic submicroscopic events, without any suggestion that he is contradicting the facts of experience. All he claims is that their stability is not static but *dynamic*. The quiet solidity of physical objects, he would say, reflects the coherence of uncountable myriads of *events* at the atomic or subatomic level, each of which by itself might seem almost unrelated to its neighbours in space or time.

For another and rather different illustration of dynamic stability,[5] ask a television engineer to explain the patterns of light and shade that form the image on the face of a TV tube, say when we are watching the Trooping of the Colour. All that is happening on the screen, he will assure us, is but a succession of isolated sparks of light produced by electron-impact; yet because of the regularities in the *programme* of signals controlling the intensity of the beam of electrons, these sparks fall into a coherent pattern, forming stable images of the objects we are watching. Whether the scene is one of violent change or of perfect calm, or indeed whether it continues in being at all, depends entirely on the modulating programme. Any stability the picture has is a dynamic or contingent stability, conditional on the maintenance in being and the coherence of the succession of event-giving signals.

Perhaps a still better example for our purpose would be

[5] Donald M. MacKay, *The Clockwork Image*, Inter-Varsity Press, London, 1974, ch. 6.

the kind of 'television tennis game' that modern electronics has made possible, where the players can control the movement of various objects appearing on a TV screen by means of the knobs and switches on a 'black box' in their own living-room. Here again, the 'ball' and the 'bat' are dynamically stable patches of light held in being by a coherent succession of control signals, and moved around the screen by changing the timing of these control signals. But in this case what we are watching is not a representation of the real world as seen through some distant television camera. It is an *artificially created* scene, in which every object owes both its existence and its motions directly to the sustaining programme generated by the black box, as modulated by the players. Not only the contents of this synthetic world, but its laws of motion too, have dynamic rather than static stability. They are perfectly stable, for just as long as the generating programme is stable. But at the flick of a switch the contents of the synthetic world can alter completely, different laws of motion can come into operation, or the whole show can disappear without trace.

I need hardly say that none of these examples of dynamic stability is meant as an explanatory *model* of our mysterious dependence on God as portrayed in the Bible. But if we ask the writers of the Bible what makes our world tick—the sort of question that underlies any attempt to build a science of nature—we will find them using remarkably similar language. From the biblical standpoint, all the contents of our world, ourselves included, have to be 'held in being' by the continual exercise of God's sustaining power. In Christ, says Paul, 'all things were created, in heaven and on earth, visible and invisible . . . all things were created through him and for him. He is before all things, and in him *all things hold together*'.[6] Or, as the writer to the Hebrews puts it: 'In these last days [God] has spoken to us by a Son, whom he appointed the heir of all things, through whom also he created the world. He reflects the glory of God and bears the very stamp of his nature, *upholding the universe by his word of power*.'[7] For biblical theism, then, it is clear that the continuing existence of our world is not something to be taken for granted. Rather it hangs moment by moment on the continuance of the upholding word of power of its Creator, as dependent on this as the picture on a TV screen is on the maintaining programme of signals.

Not that there is any hint of unreality or illusion about the solid contents of our world—they are as real as we our-selves, as real as their Creator has conceived them to be. But their stability is nevertheless declared to be a dynamic, contingent, stability. It is only in and through the con-tinuing say-so of their and our Creator that they cohere or 'hold together'. He is the giver of being, moment by moment, to all the events in and through which we en-counter the world of physical objects, *our own bodies included*. This last point is important. Unlike the detached viewers of a television screen, we know the objects of our world by interacting with them—finding ourselves up against them, obliged to reckon with them in the space of our own agency. But however uncompromisingly realist its tone, the Bible has no room for the idea of matter as something eternally self-sufficient or indestructible. The Psalmist may praise God for the stability of the earth and the reliability of the normal links between events on which our rational expectations are based;[8] but the same Book of

    [6] Colossians 1: 16, 17 (RSV).   [7] Hebrews 1: 2, 3 (RSV).
    [8] Psalm 93: 1; 104 *passim*.

Psalms[9] speaks of a time when the earth and the heavens will perish and will be changed 'as a vesture' at the will of their Creator. In the end, for biblical theism, the only solid reality is God and what God holds in being. I hope to show that this one framework offers all the support needed both for the scientific enterprise and for the life of Christian faith.

3. *Science in a Created World*

In order to make good this claim, I suggest we begin by trying to imagine that we had never heard of modern science, and then asking ourselves what would follow if we took seriously the biblical picture of our world as dynamically stable, and dependent for its coherence on the stability of its Author's creative will. In the first place, we would obviously be urged to recognize and respond appropriately to the 'givenness' of all the twists and turns of our experience—of which more in the next two lectures. Equally we would recognize the regular succession of day and night, winter and summer, and so forth, as tokens of the coherence and stability of the creative purpose of their Giver, in which the biblical writers see evidence of God's personal faithfulness to his creatures.[10]

But there are two emphases in the Bible that would I think stand out as particularly relevant to our prospects of founding a viable scientific enterprise. First, from the Book of Genesis onward, man is commanded by his Creator to make use of ('subdue') the created order intelligently for his benefit—not (*pace* Toynbee[11]) in selfish greed, but in a spirit of gratitude and responsible stewardship[12] and reverent admiration for its Giver.[13] Loving the Lord our

---

9 Psalm 102: 25–7. 10 Genesis 8: 22; Psalm 104. 11 Loc. cit.
12 Genesis 1: 28–30. 13 Psalm 111: 2.

God with all our mind must include using our minds in a search for the patterns according to which events in his universe are reliably predictable. The more we know of these, the better the foresight we can exercise as responsible stewards. So for someone with the appropriate talents, to gain knowledge and understanding of the created order is more than a permissible human recreation; it can be a duty to its Giver, the God of all truth.

So far, so good. But just how should our minds be used to gain knowledge? Medieval scholasticism, following in the Greek tradition of Aristotle, saw the task as essentially one of teasing out the logical consequences of the definitions of the objects in the world. As Michael Foster[14] has put it, if you start from the assumption that the essence of a natural object is definable, as the essence of a geometrical object is, then you will have no more use for empirical evidence in establishing the conclusions of natural science than in establishing the conclusions of Euclidean geometry. This is not to say that sensory experience played no part in ancient science, but that it played a different part: it supplied the *illustration* but not the *evidence* of the conclusions of science.

And here we come up against the second key emphasis in biblical theism. The God of the Bible is no mere craftsman, shaping pre-existing matter into forms definable *a priori* in abstract terms. He is a free and unconditioned *Creator*: the Giver of being to a world of his own devising whose nature could neither be defined nor fully deduced by reference to any first principles.[15]

---

[14] M. B. Foster, 'The Christian Doctrine of Creation and the Rise of Modern Natural Science', *Mind*, 43 (1934), pp. 446–68.

[15] To quote Michael Foster again: 'The voluntary activity of the Creator (i.e. that in his activity which exceeds determination by reason) terminates

Of such a world, knowledge by logical deduction from definitions is out. Only sensory experience can offer a valid basis for natural science. To us nowadays this conclusion may seem so obvious as hardly to need stating; but this only shows how complete was the eventual victory of the Hebraic doctrine of God and nature over the scornful opposition of the Graeco-medieval tradition. The point for the moment is that biblical theism, by denying that we can lay down in advance what the world ought to be like, offers positive encouragement to the experimental approach to nature that we now take for granted as 'scientific'. The history of the rise of modern science amply illustrates the crucial effect of this doctrine in liberating and inspiring the pioneers of empirical investigation.[16]

4. *'Customs of the Creator'*

So far, we have seen that anyone who takes biblical theism seriously will have a strong incentive to gain systematic knowledge of his world, and to do so by meticulous and unprejudiced observation rather than by working out in advance the way things 'ought' to be. A Sovereign Creator is not to be tied by what his human creatures judge to be 'reasonable'. But if we were to stop there, the prospect for our science might seem rather bleak: a matter of endless, patient description, with no hint of explanation other than the inscrutable will of the Creator. With such a God surely

on the *contingent* being of the creature (i.e. on that element of its being which eludes determination by form, namely its matter and the characteristics which it possesses *qua* material). If such voluntary activity is essential to God, it follows that the element of contingency is essential to what He creates.' (Loc. cit., p. 464.)

[16] R. Hooykaas, *Religion and the Rise of Modern Science*, Scottish Academic Press and Chatto & Windus, 1972.

anything might happen? What hope could there be of our making coherent sense of the pattern of events?

To this question one obvious answer is 'Well, why not try it, and see?'; but there are also important grounds for optimism in what the Bible itself has to say about the *character* of God. The biblical Creator may be all-powerful, and answerable to none of his creatures; but he is not capricious. He is the God of order, dependability, faithfulness. So our theistic scientist would certainly have an incentive at least to look for, if not to predict, a corresponding orderliness in the pattern of observed events in the created world.

As we all know, this adventure of faith has been rewarded beyond the wildest dreams of those who launched it in the sixteenth and seventeenth centuries. The pattern of natural events has turned out to have a marvellously intelligible structure. The regularities—the 'customs of the Creator' as they were called by the pioneers—are of two kinds. The first and most obvious are those of simple succession or co-occurrence: night follows day, summer follows winter, the sun reaches its zenith simultaneously at points on the same meridian; but we would not speak of one of these pairs of events as a *cause* of the other. The second kind of regularity we call *causal*. Crop failure follows drought, intoxication follows over-indulgence in alcohol, thunder follows the discharge of lightning. The challenge to the scientist is to discover what he calls the 'mechanism' underlying these observed correlations. In the case of thunder, for example, he will talk of electrical discharge producing heat; heat producing sudden expansion of the air; sudden expansion producing a shock wave; and so on. Each link in that chain represents a more general type of correlation which has been observed often enough to be taken for granted. If we are not content to take these correlations for granted, more detailed 'mechanisms' can be sketched which exhibit each as the resultant of a still finer chain-mesh of cause-and-effect. Ultimately, the scientist's aim is to find a set of general principles so comprehensive that all such causal sequences can be recognized as instances or combinations of a few basic kinds of regularity. Such basic principles, established by long enough precedent under sufficiently testing conditions, tend to be called 'laws of nature'; an event is said to be 'explained' scientifically if we can show that it *conforms to the general precedent* expressed in such 'laws'. In effect, to explain something scientifically means to show that it *ought not to have surprised* anyone who knew the initial conditions and the general customs of the Creator.

In these terms a scientific *theory* of a phenomenon is an attempt to link together expectations based on accepted general precedent, in such a way that (if the theory is sufficiently 'deterministic') all future instances of the phenomenon can be recognized (at least in principle) as what *ought to have been expected* by a sufficiently well-informed observer. 'Nothing else *could have* happened', we sometimes say; but what we mean—or what we are strictly justified in meaning—is only that nothing else could have been expected on the basis of precedent. In *our explanatory model* of the situation, only one thing could have happened in those circumstances; but in the end it is for reality to call the tune.

In this sense, although scientific laws do not make things happen, they do more than just describe the way things happen. They also *prescribe* the expectations that would be rational on the basis of precedent. To develop such a theory of the connections between events is, from a biblical standpoint, an act of stewardship that should help men to serve their Creator more effectively. To neglect to do so would be to fail in our religious duty.

5. *Two Questions*

Starting from a basis in the biblical doctrine of God and nature, we have reached a point at which the whole enterprise of experimental science emerges as an expression of Christian responsibility, with no hint of tension between the two. But before we go further there are two questions that you may feel inclined to raise.

First, does not the idea of *looking for a precedent* for a particular created event in terms of earlier created events presuppose that the Creator is *bound* in some way by precedent? How does this square with the idea that he is free and sovereign? The biblical answer is that the Creator has freely undertaken the creation of 'a cosmos, not a chaos'. He is certainly under no *obligation* to maintain precedent; but he encourages us to believe that his sustaining activity actually has both structure and purpose, some of it intelligible enough to be grasped by even our finite minds. The biblical data leave entirely open to investigation the nature and extent of this intelligible structure. As we shall see in the next lecture, there may be fundamental limits to our ability to predict the future on the basis of precedent; and Christianity need have no more stakes in deterministic than in indeterministic theories of the physical world. But in any case a God who was *bound* to conform to observed precedent in all circumstances would not be the sovereign Creator spoken of in the Bible.

A second question would certainly be pressed by those who see science as undermining Christian faith today. Whatever its status in theory, they might say, is not scientific explanation in practice an *alternative* to a religious understanding of events? Obviously in one sense for many of our contemporaries the answer is 'yes'. If the biblical theistic picture is correct, the scientific game of linking events into 'causal chains' can (and indeed should) proceed without bringing in 'God' as one of the links in the chain. For the theist, God comes in as the Giver of all the events, not just as a special kind of link between some of them. It is therefore technically possible to practise science in complete forgetfulness of the One who, according to the Bible, alone gives being to the data, and grounds for the expectations based on them. There is a 'proper secularisation' of science, as R. Hooykaas[17] has put it, even from a biblical standpoint.

What is completely unjustified, however, is the suggestion that successful scientific explanation rationally warrants *disbelief* in the Creator. This would be as illogical as to suggest that finding a causal connection between the impact of the 'bat' and the motion of the 'ball' in the television tennis game eliminates any need for the black box as the sustainer-in-being of the whole show. Explanations in terms of links *within* a created world are logically not in contradiction with, but complementary to, explanations in terms of the power and purpose of the Creator of that world. If, moreover, as the Bible declares, our Creator has a personal purpose in bringing each of *us* into being— a purpose with which our whole eternal destiny is linked— then to ignore this on grounds of our satisfaction with scientific explanations would be totally irrational and ultimately self-destructive.

[17] R. Hooykaas, *The Christian Approach in Teaching Science*, Tyndale Press, London, 1960, p. 10.

6. *Miracle*

Our argument so far has been running pretty much one way. There are biblical grounds for expecting the normal pattern of God's sustaining activity to conform to precedent, and in that sense to be scientifically explicable. To discover such explanations does nothing to diminish the direct dependence of the events in question upon God. So far, so good. But the Christian faith also recognizes the category of *miracle*. How does this fit into the picture we have been developing?

There is a sense in which, if the picture is true, every natural event is a miracle: an act of God so marvellous that as John Donne[18] put it 'only the daily doing takes off the admiration'. But in biblical parlance the term stands for an event that departs from the ordinary run in such a way as to communicate God's personal concern with the situation, and his sovereignty in it. This need not always mean a violation of the precedent we call 'natural'. The drying up of the Red Sea to allow the Israelites to cross could be regarded as miraculous in its timing, whether or not the east wind had a 'natural' explanation. On the other hand, the resurrection of Christ is presented as a unique event with no claim whatsoever to fit with natural precedent. The one who had been done to death was none other than the Creator himself; so, as Peter argues, 'it could not be that death should keep him in its grip'.[19] For such an unprecedented event there could be no rational incentive to seek explanations in terms of precedent.

In our day, as it happens, the swing against science has brought with it so much irrationality and credulity that

[18] John Donne, *Eighty Sermons*, no. 22, 1640. Cited in R. Hooykaas, *The Principle of Uniformity in Geology, Biology and Theology*, Brill, Leiden, 1963, p. 225.   [19] Acts 2: 24 (NEB).

this aspect of biblical Christianity is in danger of being mis-perceived. Spoon-benders and occultists delight to mock the staid conventionality of orthodox physics, and there are signs that miracle in the biblical sense is liable to be regarded as in much the same quasi-magical category— even becoming more socially acceptable in some circles as a result. Christians who are tempted to grind apologetic axes on alleged evidence for the 'paranormal' must, how-ever, remember two things. First, if a God who holds in being a dynamically stable world has reason to bring about a unique and unprecedented event, he can do so as easily as you or I could change the pattern of an artificially created sequence on a TV screen, quite regardless of the regularity with which precedent has been observed in the past. It would make no sense to speak of him as 'using hitherto undiscovered laws' to bring it about, since he has merely to say the word, and it is done.[20] To try to make such an event respectable as an instance of a standard class of phenomena called 'paranormal' (which if only we knew enough we could bring about ourselves) would be woefully to mistake its character.

Secondly, it is vital to recognize that the biblical concept of miracle is poles apart from the irrational and the in-coherent. What is stressed in the Bible is rather the *fitting-ness* of a miraculous event, as seen by its Creator, given the circumstances and his concern for those involved. So Peter presents the resurrection of Christ not as a mere magician's act designed to awe us by its inexplicability, but as *what was only to be expected*, given the awesome fact of who Christ was. Such a claim would be only side-tracked, and in no way supported, by any suggestion that the event might 'conform to established paranormal precedents'.

[20] Psalm 33: 9.

This is perhaps the point at which to express some misgivings about the common use of the (non-biblical) term 'supernatural' to refer to the miraculous. If all it means is 'unprecedented', this is harmless enough; but the term has pagan overtones that can cause confusion. The danger is that it lends credence to a thought-model (derived from ancient Greek sources rather than the Bible) in which 'nature' has a self-sustaining power independent of God, and miracle happens when God 'intervenes' by exerting a superior power. For biblical theism, the miraculous is not so much an intervention (since God's sustaining activity is never absent) as a *change of mode* of the divine agency.

7. *Objectivity*

We have been trying to work out what it should be like to serve as a scientist in God's world; to take one's mandate for the scientific enterprise from the biblical view of our world and its dependence on God. Contrary to widely propagated belief, we have found nothing but encouragement to build up experimentally based knowledge into a theoretically integrated explanatory framework in which the *concept* of God, for excellent theological reasons, ought not to find an explicit use, even though the *agency* of God is the ground of being of the whole subject-matter. Of 'irreconcilable contradiction' we have found no trace.

Before ending this lecture I would like to point out one further consequence of recognizing the biblical God as the Creator of our space-time. Philosophers of science understandably argue as to how objective our scientific knowledge can claim to be. Relativity Theory, as we shall see in the third lecture, has cast doubt on the idea that one single description of the universe can be completely valid for all observers. Quantum theory in turn challenges the distinction between the observer and the observed. Psychology and sociology have each their own reasons for voicing similar doubts. In face of all this it has proved tempting to some thinkers to abandon the concept of objectivity altogether. If universal knowledge valid for all observers is unattainable, they say, should we not admit that there are as many truths as there are knowers?[21]

In the context of biblical theism such reasoning lacks cogency. Let it be admitted, at least for the sake of argument, that what I would be correct to believe about the world must differ in some particulars from what you would be correct to believe. Still, if the flood of experienced events that you and I each encounter day by day owe their being to one and the same Creator, *he* at least is in a position to know what each of us would be correct to believe, and mistaken to disbelieve, about our world. This, for the Creator, is a matter of objective fact. If he has placed you and me in different relationship to a particular situation, the *differences* between what each of us would be correct to believe about it will be equally for him a question of objective fact. True, our scientist in God's world may have no access to the Creator's-eye view of his situation; but because he knows that he is under judgement by that criterion, he is saved from the trap of confusing relativity with a denial of objectivity.

8. *Conclusion*

In summary, then, a scientist in God's world, who knows and loves the Author of it, can rejoice equally in the growth of the explanatory structure of science, and in any surprises that may shake it. For both he returns thanks to the same

---

[21] A variety of views of this kind are surveyed and criticized in *Reason and Commitment*, by Roger Trigg, Cambridge University Press, 1973.

Giver, recognizing his obligation to do justice both to the normal coherence of the flux of created events, and to its moment-by-moment contingency on the divine fiat. His mind will be open but critical, rational but not rationalistic, realizing that the God of truth is even more concerned than he is that he should not swallow falsehood—but also that he should not disbelieve what is true, however unexpected. He will be careful—especially in his public pronouncements—to distinguish as clearly as possible between data and theoretical extrapolations; chary of baseless speculation; and alert to illegitimate attempts to turn science into scient*ism*. In all this—if he can only be true to it—he may find much of value for the defence of the biblical faith; but the Christian's motive for it can never be one of apologetic expediency. His one desire must be to do the fullest justice to all the data given him by God, to whom he will be accountable for keeping the record straight.

II

The Mythology of Chance

1. The Unpredictable

IN the first lecture our emphasis was mainly on the encouragement offered by the biblical doctrine of God and nature to the exploring scientist. Everything was going his way. If you believed in a Creator who normally observes precedent in maintaining the dynamic stability of his world, it was worth while—indeed a matter of duty—to search out the regular patterns according to which events normally follow one another. Miraculous breaches of precedent could not be ruled out; but these would be so rare as to make no practical difference to the *methodology* of science. Looking for—and relying on—natural causes was not an alternative to recognizing divine agency, but a theologically justified response to its dependable character. So there was nothing necessarily anti-theistic in the famous claim of Laplace:

> Given an intelligence which could for one instant comprehend all the forces by which nature is animated and the respective situations of the beings who compose it—an intelligence sufficiently vast to submit these data to analysis—it would embrace in the same formula the movements of the greatest bodies of the universe and those of the lightest atom; for it, nothing would be uncertain, and the future, as the past, would be present to its eyes.[1]

[1] Pierre Simon Laplace, *A Philosophical Essay on Probabilities*, 6th edn., trans. F. W. Truscott and F. L. Emory, Dover, New York, 1961, p. 4.

So far, so good. But think now of the actual world of everyday events—rainstorms, breezes, an avalanche, the breaking of an ocean wave, or the simple fall of a leaf—and you will be hard put to it to find one case where a scientist would claim that in *practice* he can predict its course in full detail. 'In principle', he may murmur, 'I believe that all these things happen according to precedent; but it would be impossible in practice to make all the observations, or solve all the equations required.' So in practice we always have to leave a margin of uncertainty around our predictions, within which we say that the actual outcome is 'a matter of chance'.

Until the end of the nineteenth century we might still have believed that, given sufficient time and opportunity, this margin of uncertainty could in principle be made as small as we like. But unfortunately for such hopes, physicists at the turn of the century stumbled on a discovery that has revolutionized our whole way of thinking about small-scale events. Until then, it had been assumed that mechanistic models based on the behaviour of large-scale systems like the sun and planets should still work if 'scaled down' to atomic dimensions. But in a series of experiments in which the electrons in atoms were knocked about under controlled conditions, it became clear that one physical quantity in particular, called 'action' (energy $\times$ time), could not be scaled down without limit. Instead, the smallest change observed (or inferred) in any physical system seemed to require a minimal 'quantum' or natural unit of action. This was called Planck's Constant, and denoted by the symbol h.

The consequences for scale modelling were disastrous. Niels Bohr showed that if you wanted to model an atom as a miniature solar system, the electrons you pictured as rotating round the nucleus could occupy only certain discrete orbits, and must jump discontinuously from one to another. Worse still, the process of observation and measurement itself had to be paid for in the same units of 'action'; and this set an irreducible limit to the precision with which you could make predictions. From this Heisenberg (1926) drew the devastating conclusion that, in effect, *one-half* of all the information required for the prediction of the future from the past on the lines envisaged by Laplace must be unavailable *in principle*, and not just in practice, until after the event. As a consequence of this famous 'Uncertainty Principle' the physicists had to develop a new 'statistical' kind of mechanics, to which I referred briefly in the first lecture (p. 5). This is designed to calculate not the precise positions and speeds of atomic *particles*, but rather the relative probabilities of particular kinds of *event* called electron-impact, photon-emission, or the like. In order to calculate these probabilities physicists now talk in terms of 'probability waves' travelling from place to place, in much the same way as we talk of flu waves travelling across Europe. This does not mean that electrons or photons *are* waves—any more than flu viruses are. It means simply that the chances of the events called 'electron-impact', 'photon-emission', or 'catching flu' can be calculated using a wave-model.

But now—what do we mean here by 'chance'? Does Heisenberg's Principle mean only that such 'chance' events are *unpredictable by us*, or does it mean that they have *no determining cause*? In either case—and this is our present concern—how does all this scientific talk of 'chance' relate to the biblical conception of our world as totally dependent on the will of a sovereign God?

2. *Clearing the Ground*

In order to tackle these questions sensibly we shall have to begin by clarifying some of the ideas that cluster around the notion of chance and are often confused. To make things concrete, imagine for a start that we write down the sequence of numbers produced by tossing an ideally un-biased ten-sided die five times. If the tossing conditions could be so arranged as not to influence the way the die falls, we might call the *process* of tossing a (nearly) *random process*. The sequence of numbers might then be called a 'random sequence' purely in the sense that it is the *product* of a random process. Even if an orderly sequence such as 99999 were to turn up as a result of random tossing (we could expect several orderly sequences in every 10,000 trials) it would still be a 'random sequence' in this par-ticular sense.

Suppose, on the other hand, that the purpose of tossing the die were to produce a deliberately *disorderly* sequence— the sort of thing sometimes required in statistical experi-ments when one wants to scramble or 'randomize' the order of trials. For such a purpose the sequence 99999 or 12345 might be quite useless. We might be inclined to describe them as 'insufficiently random'—but if we did we would be using 'random' in quite a different sense, meaning 'without discernible order'. For this purpose we would do better to use a pre-printed table of well-scrambled sequences (sometimes also called 'random numbers') from which such awkward cases had been carefully weeded out.

Whenever the word 'random' is used, then, we have to ask ourselves (*a*) whether it refers to a *process* or to the *product* of that process; and if the latter, then (*b*) whether it means

Random (1)—*having no determining cause*
or Random (2)—*having no discernible order.*

This brings us to a second area of confusion, between the notions of *indeterminacy* and *unpredictability*. Strictly speaking, to call an event *unpredictable* is to say something about our science rather than the event. It means simply that our schemes of prediction had no place for it, and says nothing either way as to whether it had a determinate specification before it occurred. Even if we call it 'unpredictable in principle', we mean only that all known schemes of prediction are in principle inadequate to specify it in advance. To speak of an event as *indeterminate*, however, is to say much more than that we could not specify it beforehand. It is to say that it *had* no prior specification—that no specification existed, unknown to us, which we would have been correct to believe and mistaken to disbelieve if only we had known it.

What then would a scientist mean by a *determinate* event? Clearly it need not be one that is predictable in practice. The basic scientific question here is whether or not it had a 'determining cause'—that is, a prior event or set of events from which it followed according to precedent. If so, then given these precursors, the rules of precedent alone were logically sufficient to determine the specification of the event in every detail, including its timing, before it occurred. Thus, to take an example, future eclipses of the moon are considered (for practical purposes) 'physically determinate' events, in that their timing already has a specification which follows from the present state-description of the solar system plus the rules of precedent embodied in our astronomical theory. We specify eclipses in almanacs, not as events which are *guaranteed* to happen, but as events whose *specification* is determined according to rules of precedent we are presumed to accept. If we believe we have adequate grounds for accepting these rules, we would be irrational not to expect the events so determined.

So far we have been talking only of *determination by precedent*. This is the technical sense of 'determination' recognized in science—naturally enough, since science is the game of understanding (and where possible predicting) events on the basis of precedent. In the previous lecture, however, we found ourselves grappling with the biblical claim that the whole succession of events in the physical world is held in being by the continual agency of its Creator. We saw how, on this view, the maintenance of precedent on which science depends was attributable to the stability and coherence of the divine upholding agency. By the same token, even events which either broke with precedent, or were left undetermined by precedent, must be no less dependent on the creative fiat for their occurrence. In this context, then, we are invited to recognize a quite different notion of 'determination', namely *determination by the Giver of being*. From this standpoint events which are determined-by-precedent obviously form a subclass of events determined-by-fiat. We can set out the position diagrammatically thus:

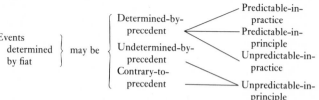

Perhaps a parochial illustration may be forgiven. In our work at Keele on the visual system we need to be able to

generate on a TV screen not only a number of movable
spots of light, as in 'TV tennis', but also patterns of '*pseudo-
random*' texture covering much of the field of view (Fig. 1).
Such patterns have equal numbers of black and white dots
distributed irregularly—rather as if one had cut up a large

FIG. 1. A 'pseudo-random' distribution of black and white dots. This specimen
is taken from B. Julesz, *Foundations of Cyclopean Perception*, University of
Chicago Press, 1971, by kind permission of the author.

chessboard pattern and shuffled the resulting pile of black
and white squares before laying them down in rows. To
produce the equivalent on a TV screen we have to arrange
for the electron beam to be switched rapidly on and off in
a pseudo-random manner as it 'paints' the pattern we want;
but if the picture is to remain stable we have to ensure that
the same sequence of blacks and whites repeats itself each
time the pattern is painted by the beam. To generate the
necessary control signals we therefore use a small piece of
computing equipment (called a 'fed back shift register')

which is essentially an electronic shuffling device designed to produce a sequence of blocks of sixteen 'ones' and 'zeros' that rings all possible changes in a fixed order before repeating itself. Since the whole process repeats 200 times per second, the result on the screen is a *dynamically stable* object whose texture *has no discernible order* (i.e. is random in sense 2) though the object can be moved around its little world coherently as a whole, and its texture is perfectly stable over time. If, however, we arrange for the sequence of signals to repeat at a rate incoherent with that at which the beam paints the picture, the result is a succession of events which are random (sense 2) in both space and time. The effect seems to be one of complete chaos—rather like the familiar 'snowstorm' seen on a TV receiver tuned to an empty channel.

The point is that despite all this 'randomness' in sense 2, the whole sequence of events on the screen is at all times precisely *determined* by the controlling generator, so it is *not* 'random' in sense 1. It is designed to be *unpredictable-in-practice*; but in fact each signal is determined by complicated rules from preceding signals, so that for anyone who knew the rules of precedence it would actually be *predictable-in-principle*. In this respect it contrasts with the TV 'snowstorm', where although the sequence of spots on the screen is also determined by the controlling signals, the sequence of those signals is *not* determined on the basis of precedent from earlier signals.

3. *Chance*

We are now in a position to look again at the questions that set us off on this ground-clearing exercise. Heisenberg's Principle as it stands is clearly a statement about *limits to our knowledge*, and not about the absence of *causal pre-cursors* for the events it declares to be uncertain. If we took the positivistic line that it is 'meaningless' to speak of a variable as determinate unless it is in principle measurable, we could of course ignore this distinction. But from any standpoint this would clearly be an arbitrary move which would 'solve' the problem only in the sense of refusing to recognize it; and from the standpoint of biblical theism it would beg the most important question of all, which is how well our view of the situation corresponds with what its Creator knows that we would be objectively correct to believe.

Interestingly enough, although Einstein was a co-founder of quantum theory through his early work on photo-electric emission, he resisted to the end any interpretation of it which, as he saw it, implied that 'God plays dice'.[2] As early as 1924 he had written to his friend Max Born: 'I find the idea quite intolerable that an electron exposed to radiation should choose of its own free will, not only its moment to jump off, but also its direction. In that case, I would rather be a cobbler, or even an employee in a gaming-house, than a physicist.'[3]

Einstein was fond of expressing his objections in quasi-theological terms. 'I like to think of the electron as *Gott* sees it', he told me once in a conversation at his home in Princeton in 1951. His meaning was clearly that if one supposed a God who knew as Creator (rather than by observation) the whole state of his world, then the distinction between epistemological uncertainty (a *lack of pre-dictive knowledge*) and ontological indeterminacy (*the*

[2] A. Einstein, Letter in *The Born-Einstein Letters*, translated by Irene Born, Macmillan, New York, 1971, p. 149.
[3] Ibid., p. 82.

absence of determining causes) was undeniably meaningful; and it was therefore illegitimate to decide merely by definition that Heisenberg's Principle implied the latter.

Thus far, Einstein was surely correct. His opponents had no rational grounds for claiming that the absence of an *observable* causal precedent for an event meant that it had *no* causal precedent. On the other hand, from a biblical standpoint it would be equally mistaken to argue that if there were no causal precursor for an event, then its Creator must be thought of as 'playing dice'. Even with human creativity there is a distinction to preserve between free creative innovation and mental coin-tossing.[4] The God of biblical theism is beholden to none to account for his creative agency. If he freely wills into being a succession of events in which one half of the sub-microscopic details at any time are unspecified by their precursors, this would involve no inconsistency with his character, still less with his sovereignty, as portrayed in the Bible. Belief in a sovereign God does not in the least entail a belief that there *must* be 'hidden physical variables' sufficient to determine the behaviour of electrons on the basis of precedent. For biblical theism all events, equally, with or without precursors according to precedent, need God's say-so in order that they occur at all. The choice of 'God or Chance' is simply not a meaningful alternative, if 'Chance' is meant in the scientific sense. As the Book of Proverbs (ch. 16, v. 33) has it: 'The lots may be cast into the lap, but the issue depends wholly on the Lord.'

There could hardly be a more explicit claim that even the events we classify technically as 'chance' or 'random'

---

[4] This is well expressed by R. J. Spilsbury in *Providence Lost: A critique of Darwinism*, Oxford University Press, London, 1974, p. 115 n.: 'Creative ideas are unpredictable, but are not the fruit of an aimed-at unpredictability.'

are determined by the sovereign Giver of their being. For biblical theism, nothing in the technical scientific idea of chance implies or requires any release of events from the sovereignty of the Creator. There is, of course, a pagan mythological notion of 'chance' as a kind of 'anti-deity', *Tyche*, the personification of chaos and meaninglessness, which biblical theism emphatically rejects. But to confuse these two concepts would be simply a blunder, or worse.

4. *A Mis-stated Issue*

On 15 March 1971 the *New York Times* splashed a headline over an exclusive interview with the biologist Jacques Monod: 'French Nobelist says a universe based on chance leaves man free to choose his own ethical values.' In the book publicized by the interview, Monod pulled out all the stops of French rhetoric:

'Chance *alone* is at the source of every innovation, of all creation in the biosphere. Pure chance, absolutely free but blind, at the very root of the stupendous edifice of evolution. This central concept of biology . . . is today the *sole* conceivable hypothesis, the only one compatible with observed and tested fact.' 'The biosphere looks like the product of a unique event (whose) chances of occurring were almost nil. . . . The universe was not pregnant with life. . . . Our number came up in the Monte Carlo game.' It is on these grounds that Monod delivers the judgement I quoted at the beginning of these lectures, claiming that 'man at last knows that he is alone in the unfeeling immensity of the universe, out of which he emerged only by chance'. All forms of life, he told his interviewer, are the product of 'pure chance'. 'These discoveries . . . make it impossible to accept any system . . . that assumes a master plan of creation.'[5]

Now according to the leaflet advertising his book, 'Monod uses the unrelenting logic of the scientist . . . to demolish traditional forms of philosophy.' So I hope it is not unfair to examine briefly the logic of the conclusions he claims to draw from science *vis-à-vis* the biblical theistic position in particular. To clear the air, let us imagine that all Monod's scientific premises were granted, and translate them into the now familiar terms. The collision between minuscule particles of nucleic acid and protein in the 'prebiotic soup', which he claims initiated the evolution of living forms, was a 'chance' event. Very well, suppose it was. If this is meant as a statement based on *scientific evidence*, the most it can imply is that this fateful event did not follow according to law-like precedent from any assignable precursor (or more weakly, that it was highly improbable on the basis of prior conditions). This may indeed upset any who thought that the evolution of species was something as predictable as the unfolding of one of those lovely Japanese paper flowers in water; and I make no judgement as to who is right. But what one wants to ask Monod is—*what is all the theological fuss about?* Where, in biblical theism, is anything said or implied to the contrary of his scientific hypothesis?

We might suspect some conflict with the first chapter of Genesis; but whatever our interpretation of the mysterious language used there, it would be hard to pretend that it comes down in favour of causal continuity rather than discontinuity in the physical processes that set off the biological train. 'Then God said, "Let the earth produce fresh growth,

    [5] Jacques Monod, *Chance and Necessity*, Collins, London, 1972, pp. 110, 136, 137, 167.

let there be on the earth plants bearing seed, fruit-trees bearing fruit each . . . according to its kind. . . ." God said, "Let the earth bring forth living creatures, according to their kind: cattle, reptiles, and wild animals, all according to their kind".'[6]

The plain truth is (and Monod fails to cite any evidence to the contrary) that nothing in the Bible offers even indirect evidence for or against the hypothesis that life originated in an event which was unforeseeable on the basis of scientific precedent—a hypothesis, he tells us, which 'makes it impossible' to believe in 'a master plan of creation'. Whether we as scientists would classify an event as 'chance' or as 'physically determinate' is of no concern whatever to the biblical writers, who would coolly assure us that God gives being to all events in both categories, and that he is sovereign equally over either category. Monod's notion of a 'master plan' may actually not be the best description of what the Bible refers to as God's 'eternal purpose'. Without careful qualification it might sound more Platonic than biblical.[7] But certainly the concept of divine sovereignty in physical events as exemplified in the Bible has no quarrel whatsoever with a hypothesis that some of these events were extremely improbable by human reckoning. This much is clear whether one believes in either, or neither.

What then has misled Monod into telling his hundreds of thousands of readers the very opposite? He appears to have fallen straight (though perhaps not unwillingly) into the trap we noted earlier, of confusing the scientific and the mythological concepts of 'chance'. 'Chance' in science is not the name of a thing or an agent, least of all of a *cause*

[6] Genesis 1: 11, 24 (NEB).

[7] For a penetrating analysis of the contrasts between biblical and Greek concepts of creation, see Foster, loc. cit., pp. 439–66.

or *source* of anything; it stands for the *absence* of an assignable cause.

'I see nobody on the road', said Alice. 'I only wish *I* had such eyes', the King remarked in a fretful tone. 'To be able to see Nobody! And at that distance too.' . . . 'Who did you pass on the road?' the King went on, holding out his hand to the Messenger for some more hay. 'Nobody', said the Messenger. 'Quite right', said the King: 'this young lady saw him too. So of course Nobody walks slower than you.' 'I do my best', the Messenger said in a sullen tone. 'I'm sure nobody walks much faster than I do!' 'He can't do that', said the King, 'or else he'd have been here first.'[8]

To personify 'chance' as if we were talking about a causal agent, 'free but blind' and the rest is more than harmless poetic effluvium: it is to make an illegitimate switch from a *scientific* to a quasi-religious *mythological* concept. To proceed to claim scientific authority for describing *this* as a 'central concept of biology' is to compound confusion. To dress up the result as if it were 'observed and tested fact' that was at odds with all concepts of divine immanence in natural events is little short of dishonest.

Monod's astonishingly ill-supported argument is probably not to be understood apart from his declared hatred of all forms of religion, which he scorns as 'rooted in animism, [existing] outside objective knowledge, outside truth, and . . . strangers and fundamentally hostile to science, which they are willing to use but do not respect or cherish' (loc. cit., p. 159). This leaves little doubt as to the 'hostility' on Monod's side! Whether the details of his accusation truthfully describe the biblical theism we have been studying I must leave my readers to judge.

[8] Lewis Carroll, *Alice through the Looking Glass*, ch. vii.

To be fair, it should be said that some would-be defenders of the faith must share part of the blame for the confusion that vitiates Monod's anti-theistic argument from 'chance'. This is not because they were too faithful to the Bible, but rather because they were not faithful enough: their thinking failed to give due place to the biblical emphasis on the sovereignty of God. The apologetic literature of the last hundred years has all too many examples where Christian theologians seem to have been trapped into tacitly agreeing with their opponents in confusing the technical and the metaphysical concepts of 'chance', and imagining that to classify an event or process scientifically as 'random' would prevent or at least excuse anyone from recognizing the hand of God in it. Instead of attacking this presupposition as a misinterpretation of the biblical position, these theologians actually strengthened it by trying to pick scientific holes in evolutionary theories that attributed the origins of species to 'chance' processes—thus giving the impression that the credibility of the Christian doctrine of creation depended on their success. Their reaction is perhaps understandable enough when we find evolutionary authorities like G. G. Simpson claiming in the name of science that 'man is the result of a purposeless and materialistic process that did not have him in mind. He was not planned.'[9] It may also be true that in our day evolutionary theories are too uncritically swallowed and too dogmatically propagated for the health of science; and one factor in this unhealthy lowering of critical scientific standards may have been a fear in some quarters that the only alternative would be to invoke a miracle. If so, one must hope that technically qualified scientists, whether Christian or not, will have the

[9] G. G. Simpson, *The Meaning of Evolution*, Yale University Press, New Haven, 1949, p. 344.

courage to set the scientific balance right as a matter of professional duty. But for Christian theologians as such to assume a vested interest in the outcome of the technical debate would be to go well beyond their biblical brief.

5. *The Winding-down of the World?*

No discussion of the theology of chance could be complete without some mention of the famous Second Law of Thermodynamics. This states that in a closed system the over-all disorder must increase towards a maximum as time goes on. There are complications about the definition of disorder, the possibility of brief fluctuations in the opposite direction, and so forth; but broadly speaking this is an accepted Law of Nature. The physicist's index of disorder is called *entropy*, which measures in effect the amount of information that would be needed in order to specify precisely how the total energy is distributed throughout the system in question. The higher the entropy, the more 'scrambled' is the distribution of energy, and the more questions remain to be answered.

As it happens, communication engineers and physicists have recently found ways of defining the notion of 'amount of information' in very similar mathematical terms to those used to define entropy.[10] Where a message identifies one out of two equally likely possibilities, the information received is defined as one unit or 'bit'. To identify one out of four equally likely possibilities (2×2) requires two bits; one out of eight ($2 \times 2 \times 2$) three bits: and so on. So information, for the communication engineer, is '*that which resolves uncertainty*'; and he measures it by the mathematical

---

[10] C. E. Shannon and W. Weaver, *The Mathematical Theory of Communication*, University of Illinois Press, 1949, and D. M. MacKay, *Information, Mechanism and Meaning*, M.I.T. Press, Cambridge, Mass., 1969.

'unforeseeableness' (strictly the logarithm of the improb-
ability) of the answer it brings. This allows us to describe
the Second Law of Thermodynamics in an intuitively
simple form: the amount of information (number of bits)
required to specify the precise microstate of an isolated
system increases to a maximum as time goes on. In other
words, if you start with a partly specified closed system,
the energy within it gets redistributed in such a way that
your uncertainty as to its precise state can only increase as
time goes on. What gives practical importance to all this
is that energy can be made to do work in a system only if
we know how it is distributed; so it is not surprising that
the Second Law made its first appearance in the theory of
steam-engines. Yet despite these severely practical origins
it has found itself invoked in two of the classical areas of
past debate between scientists and theologians.

The first is once again the theory of evolution. Evolu-
tionists maintain that more highly ordered forms of life
evolved out of simpler forms. Anti-evolutionists (even up
to the present time) have tried to argue that this conflicts
with both the spirit and the letter of the Second Law of
Thermodynamics. This, however, will not do. The earth
is not an isolated system. It receives a continual flood of
highly ordered energy from the sun; and if one estimates
the resulting increase in entropy (energy disorder) for the
sun, this vastly outweighs any local reduction in energy
disorder brought about on earth by biological processes,
whether evolutionary or otherwise. It is possible, of course,
to ask questions from the standpoint of Information Theory
itself as to the likelihood that enough information (in the
technical sense) could have been generated in a few hundred
million years of random trial-and-error to specify the
marvellously intricate structures of living organisms. This,

however, is a separate issue from the thermodynamic one, and is still hotly debated.[11]

The second area of debate concerns the so-called 'heat death of the universe'. The Second Law predicts that any *closed* system will tend finally towards an equilibrium in which all parts will have the same (probably very low) temperature. Apply this to the whole universe, and you have a prediction of the End of the World, not in either a bang or a whimper, but in icy nothingness. Many fine sagas have been written by scientific journalists on this theme, which undeniably stirs the imagination.

But is it science? What the myth makers have to assume here is that in the technical sense of the Second Law the universe is a *closed system*. Unfortunately this seems an unprovable assumption. Scientific theories of 'continuous creation' come and go, and no existing evidence (some would say no conceivable evidence) can rule out speculations that the orderliness of the universe is continuously replenished, or even oscillates up and down over some long time scale.[12]

The basic point here is that all talk of 'probability' is *relative*. The probability of an event depends on the evidence available to the knower. If I offer to read out to you the sequence of digits down the right-hand column of our local telephone directory, the probability-for-you that the last digit (or any digit) will be 9 may be 1 in 10. But for the people at the exchange every digit is fully specified,

[11] L. M. Spetner, 'Natural Selection: An Information-Transmission Mechanism for Evolution', *J. Theoret. Biol.* 7 (1964), pp. 412–19; 'A New Look at the Theory of Evolution', in *Challenge: Torah Views on Science and its Problems*, edited by A. Carmell and C. Domb, Feldheim Publishers, Jerusalem–New York, 1976; P. S. Moorhead and M. M. Kaplan (eds.), *Mathematical Challenges to the Neo-Darwinian Interpretation of Evolution*, Wister Inst. Monog. No. 5, Philadelphia, 1967.

[12] See, for example, W. J. Kaufmann III, *Relativity and Cosmology* (2nd edn.), Harper & Row, New York, 1977.

and talk of 'probability' would be pointless. (Incidentally, this example illustrates nicely the fallacy of confusing the two senses of 'randomness' (p. 25). The sequence of digits is quite random in sense 2. As a numerical sequence it has no discernible order. But anyone who on these grounds were to describe it as 'meaningless' or 'purposeless', or 'random' in sense 1, would be simply missing the point. It is in fact so highly ordered that not a single misprint could be tolerated.)

To speak of the entropy of the whole universe brings up a similar problem. Entropy is defined in terms of probabilities. The definition presupposes that the detailed state of the system is not fully specified. If we take seriously the concept of a sovereign Creator, however, any talk of 'probability' for him must be beside the point. He knows all. There can be no rational grounds for holding that he is bound or limited by the Second Law.

In short, the data of science leave entirely open the future course of the cosmic drama. The Second Law of Thermodynamics can do no more than assure us that a gradual winding down of the universe is one of the possible Last Acts. If the drama is actually held in being by a divine Author, of course, the Last Act may be different from our wildest imaginings.

6. *Conclusion*

We have pursued the theme of 'chance' in its scientific sense from the sub-microscopic level of atomic events to the cosmic level at which men contemplate the future of the universe. Our analysis has, I hope, made it clear that for science as such the term has a strictly defined and theologically innocent function. It denotes simply *what defies determination on the basis of precedent*. It is the scientist's name for the unforeseeable, not the meaningless. As such it implies no resistance whatsoever to the biblical doctrine that even in the case of the most scientifically inscrutable event, 'the whole disposing thereof is of the Lord'. For the biblical writers it is unquestionable that the Holder-in-being of this strange drama in which we find ourselves has ultimate sovereignty, no less over its unforeseen twists and turns than over its scientifically predictable stretches.

Superficially, it may seem meaningful to ask of a particular event whether it was due to the agency of God or to chance. But if the God we are talking about is the God whom Christians worship as Creator and Sustainer of the Universe, this is strictly a *non-question*. To speak of 'leaving something to chance', if it means anything more than just 'leaving something to happen', must mean simply 'leaving it to the will of the Creator'. It is meaningful to ask whether or not a particular event followed from precedent; and it is also meaningful (though not a scientific question) to ask whether this event betokened in a special way God's personal concern with the situation, or whether it should be accepted simply as part of his normal 'care and maintenance'. These are real questions, not easily answered. But the question of 'God or chance' is a theological howler.

Perhaps, however, by now you may be wondering whether we have not proved too much. With a Creator so all-powerful and all-encompassing in his sovereignty, are not we, with all our concerns, reduced to the role of ineffective puppets? What room, you may ask, is left for the life of responsible dialogue with God which the Christian Scriptures portray as the chief end of our existence? To this question we must return in the concluding lecture.

III

What Room for Providence?

1. *The Image of Space–Time*

So far in these lectures we have concentrated on what the biblical writers have to say about God as Creator. We have followed the implications for the enterprise of science and found them wholly positive, if at times a little chastening. We have seen how from this standpoint the dynamic stability and lawfulness of the physical world directly reflect the coherence of the divine activity in which we and our world 'live and move and have our being'.

But all this may seem to have little room for something that is surely of the essence of biblical religion. The God of Abraham, of the prophets and the psalmists, and supremely of Christ and his apostles, is One whom men can come to know and love. He stands at the door and knocks, and promises that, if anyone will open the door, 'I will come in to him and will sup with him, and he with me.'[1] What kind of talk is this? Have we not in the last two lectures been insisting that God-as-Creator is not to be pictured as an invisible inhabitant of our world: it is rather our world that has its being in *him*. But if so, how can we his creatures ever come to *know* our Creator?

The answer of Christian theism is that this would be quite impossible were it not that God himself takes the initiative

[1] Revelation 3: 20 (AV).

to reveal something of himself in the experienced events of his created world.

In order to try to think coherently about this, I find some help in another image that comes out of modern science itself. Relativity theory, backed by numerous observations on high-speed particles and the like, has taught us to regard time as one of the dimensions of our world in somewhat the same sense as length, breadth, and height. When the four are combined the whole of our existence, past, present, and future, can be imagined as an extended 4-dimensional pattern of events: a 'space–time'. It is this whole space–time that in biblical terms is God's creation.

Dorothy Sayers[2] has likened the creation of such a space–time to the human act of creating a novel or a drama. The author's conception encompasses the past, present, and future of his creation in a single imaginative exercise. This exercise may occupy a stretch of the author's lifetime, measurable in (his) hours or days; but the time-scale on which these days are marked is logically quite distinct from the time-scale of the created world of the novel. Its creation is not an event among the events of that world. Rather do all those events have their being *in* the one creative act, which relative to them is 'timeless' or 'eternal'.

In this sense, then, the dimensions in which the author of a space–time has his being *transcend* those of that space–time. If this is so for ordinary human authorship, then all the more must we be prepared for it to limit our ability to think about God as the Author of our space–time. I do not mean that this or any human analogy can be at all an adequate model; but it does at least warn us that the being of such a God must be expected to transcend the $(3+1)$-

---

[2] Dorothy Sayers, *Unpopular Opinions*, Gollancz, 1946, pp. 53–6. Also *The Mind of the Maker*, Methuen, 1941.

dimensionality of our world. In that case, no single representation in the concepts of our space-time could be dimensionally adequate to depict him, any more than a single 2-dimensional drawing can do justice to a 3-dimensional girder bridge.

But perhaps the case of the girder bridge offers a glimmer of hope. What the draughtsman does in such a case is to use what he calls *projections*: 2-dimensional drawings which reveal *all that is to be seen* of the bridge from one direction at a time. An object with more than two dimensions needs *more than one* such projection, preferably from directions at right angles, in order to begin to do justice to its structure. When we turn to the classical Christian theologians we find them saying some strikingly similar things about the being of God and the inadequacy of human images to do him justice. God is personal—yes, but his multidimensional being is such that not one but *three* personal 'projections' are necessary to begin to do justice to what he has revealed about himself. The Divine Being has as it were three personal 'faces'. 'The Father is God, The Son is God; and the Holy Ghost is God. And yet they are not three Gods: but one God.'[3]

2. *What Makes a Contradiction?*

Confronted with such a statement out of context any logically minded reader might be excused for protesting, if not stopping his ears and flying for his sanity. What is going on? Is this not abusing all the canons of logic? I must confess that at one time I was inclined to be impatient with talk of this kind. My trouble, I think, was that I had too simplistic an idea of what makes a logical contradiction. Let me explain what I mean with the help of a familiar

[3] *The Athanasian Creed.*

illustration. Hold up a finger and thumb, one 5 or 10 cm behind the other, in line with your nose. Now close each eye in turn. With one eye, you see the finger to the left of the thumb; with the other, to the right. Verbally this sounds like a contradiction. But if you now open both eyes, you have a different kind of experience: you see-in-depth a single finger, displaced from the thumb in a *third dimension*. The point is a very simple one. When you are confronted with a situation which has more dimensions than your descriptive framework, you must be prepared to accept and seek to integrate more than one description, from more than one standpoint, if you are not to miss some of the truth about that situation; and you must expect in general to find *systematic disparities* between these descriptions. They are not logically contradictory, but complementary. In the case of binocular vision it is precisely the disparities between left- and right-eye views that give us information about the depth-dimension which is missing from (because at right angles to) the 2-dimensional images thrown on to the retinae of our eyes.[4]

The moral for our present discussion is twofold. First, since the Being of God is a complete mystery to us apart from what he may disclose to us, our only hope of learning of its 'dimensionality' must be through careful and unprejudiced integration of any images he may offer us in human terms, *being specially careful to preserve the disparities* between different images, as the chief source of clues to the 'depths' of what is to be perceived. Secondly, before trying to make sense of any statement about God, it is essential to identify as well as we can the *standpoint* for which it claims to be a valid 'projection'. By the same token, before dismiss-

[4] B. Julesz, *Foundations of Cyclopean Perception*, University of Chicago Press, 1971.

ing two verbally disparate theological statements as 'conflicting', it is essential to establish that they are not framed
for different standpoints, and so logically complementary.[5]

There is a further and more general lesson to be drawn
from our simple example. The integration of left- and
right-eye views to give us the experience of seeing-in-depth
is something that our visual nervous system is well equipped
to achieve, but you and I would find it hard to *specify in
words*. For an extreme illustration of this point, try another

FIG. 2. If these pictures are viewed with the eyes crossed (or in a stereoscope) so
that the two images seem to coincide, the disparities between them reveal a
'camouflaged' square, standing out in depth. (Adapted from Julesz, loc. cit.)

experiment. Cut out a small square of sandpaper, and
support it a few centimetres in front of a sheet of the same
material. Viewed with either the left or right eye alone,
the square will be perfectly camouflaged and undetectable
against its background. Viewed with both eyes simultaneously, however, it stands out in depth and is easily
seen. The two photographs in Fig. 2 show left- and

[5] D. M. MacKay, 'Complementarity in Scientific and Theological Thinking',
Zygon, **9**, no. 3 (1974), pp. 225-44.

right-eye views of such a camouflaged square. By cross-
ing one's eyes so that the two images appear to lie on
top of one another (or viewing the two pictures in a
stereoscope) one can easily see the square 'in relief' against
its background; yet no hint of its existence is given by either
picture alone.

With more complex 3-dimensional camouflaged surfaces
it may take some time before their shape 'clicks' into perception.[6] Until it does, the images from the two eyes 'fight'
in what the psychologist calls 'binocular rivalry'. If I have
difficulties in fusing the two to form the single 3-dimensional
image that others are talking about, a friend may be able
to help me by telling me what to look for; but in the end
the process of integration has to happen within my own
nervous system, and the wrong 'perceptual set' may post-
pone this indefinitely. Moreover, no amount of intellectual
understanding of his description can be equivalent to the
perceptual experience. If I want to know for myself what
he is talking about, a change has to happen in *me*. Note also
that despite the subjective flavour of all this, there is nothing
optional about the reality of the camouflaged surface. It is
objectively *there to be reckoned with*. I am not being invited
to persuade myself into seeing something illusory, but
rather to remove the psychological barriers that prevent
me from seeing things as they actually are.

The lesson for our present purpose scarcely needs spell-
ing out. If we are to do justice to what the biblical writers
claim to be self-disclosures by God in various circumstances—to perceive what is there to be perceived in and
through the data—then not only must we be patient of
apparent disparities; we must also be prepared for some
time to pass, and maybe much effort to be expended, before

[6] Julesz, loc. cit.

our perception begins to 'click'. We must not be surprised if friends who claim to 'see it' are able to help us relatively little by what they say, however hard and lovingly they try. We must recognize and actively guard against the danger that a wrong 'perceptual set' may blind us to what is objectively there to be seen, just as much as the danger of deluding ourselves into 'wishful thinking'. Above all, we must be prepared for the integration of the evidence to take place in us as whole human beings, and not merely in our minds at the level of verbal reasoning.

What then distinguishes a genuine contradiction—the 'untruth' that the Bible abhors—from the kind of revealing disparity we have been discussing? The key question is whether the disparity goes with a *difference of standpoint*. Two disparate accounts from exactly the same standpoint cannot both be true. But if two accounts are framed from different standpoints, disparity between them is not necessarily evidence of untruth (indeed in such a case an *absence* of disparity might sometimes indicate a falsehood).

I am afraid I know of no procedure for infallibly identifying the logical standpoint of an account; but the general idea of a *difference* in standpoint is clear enough from the example of left- and right-eye views. Each eye is in a definably different (geometrical) *relation to the subject-matter*, and the two relations *are mutually exclusive.*[7] So anyone who claims that two disparate accounts are framed for different standpoints ought at least to be prepared to say in what respect the 'preconditions of use' of the one exclude at least one precondition of use of the other. To this point we shall return.

[7] MacKay, loc. cit.

3. *The Human Face of God*

We can now look at the range and variety of biblical statements about God in a new light. Because the being of a
Creator transcends the dimensionality of his created space-
time, the most we could hope for by way of a description of
God would be a succession of 'projections' of one aspect
at a time in our human 3-dimensional categories, each
showing us something of the relationship between us and
our Creator from one particular 'angle'. Disparities between
such projections, if they are genuine, are to be welcomed
as informative clues; but we need not expect to be able to
resolve them into an integrated multidimensional picture
just by thinking about them. Our minds find it hard enough
to do this kind of exercise even for 2-dimensional drawings
of 3-dimensional objects. The example of binocular vision
suggests that our best hope of achieving some integration
will be to absorb what we can of each projection *when we
ourselves are in the appropriate situation* for that projection,
and to avoid the mistake of trying to absorb a projection
'from the wrong angle'—i.e. in a situation for which that
projection does not apply.

As with physical Relativity Theory, this can be a tough
mental discipline. Our instinct is to feel that wherever we
may be, we ought to 'make the fullest use of all information', and that to ignore any projection in a given situation
would be irrational. But even the case of binocular vision
shows that the opposite can actually be the case. If we want
to see-in-depth, it is essential to ensure that each eye sees
only the view appropriate to its situation, and not the other.
To rig up a system of mirrors so that both left- and right-
eye views were projected into the same eye would be sense-
less. It would simply generate a perceptual pseudo-conflict

and frustrate the integration we say we want to achieve. The basic point is that with a multidimensional situation the projection from one standpoint *is not valid information* from another (exclusive) standpoint.

Is it possible then to 'sort for standpoint' the diverse ways in which the Bible speaks of God, so that we may avoid this frustrating mistake, and can hope to make some integrated operational sense of what it sets before us? Let there be no false hopes. We have no encouragement to believe that our understanding can encompass God— quite the reverse. But if we are assured that the Bible contains what God wants us to understand about himself and his purpose for us,[8] then to try to open our minds to it is not a matter of pride and arrogance but of humble duty as his creatures. To neglect it, even with Uriah-Heep-like protestations, would show the reverse of humility in the eyes of the Giver of the data.

It is at this point that the image of space–time may help us. It suggests at once two fundamentally different stand-points to look for, from each of which important things may have to be said to us about our situation. One is the stand-point of the Creator-in-eternity, from which the whole of our space–time is a created fact, and time one of its dimen-sions. The other is the standpoint of us, his creatures, for whom future time is a 'becoming'.

If we approach the Bible with this distinction in our minds, many statements and images group themselves clearly into two corresponding categories. Those in one group presuppose an *extra-temporal* standpoint, from which 'one day is as a thousand years, and a thousand years as one day',[9] and all events have their being 'according to

[8] 2 Timothy 3: 16.
[9] 2 Peter 3: 8 (RSV).

the definite plan and fore-knowledge of God'.[10] The 'projection' of the being of God here revealed is clearly personal; but the Person so displayed is not one to whom we in our world can have access. We are in a created space–time, not in the eternity of the Creator. Metaphorically speaking, our 'line of sight' is in the wrong direction.

Another group of biblical statements present 'God-in-Christ' as One who meets with and addresses men *in* created space–time. In terms of our metaphor (remembering that it is only a metaphor and not a model) the biblical writers seem to be describing Christ as the fullest possible 'projection' of the being of God into our $(3+1)$-dimensional space–time. What thrills the writers of the Bible is the disclosure that in these dimensions the Being of God is *man-like*. This is presumably related to the mysterious doctrine that man is created 'in the image of God'. The metaphor of 'projection' also seems fully compatible with the New Testament description of the Son, Jesus Christ, as 'the image of the invisible God'[11] and 'the stamp of God's very being'.[12] John records how when Jesus was asked by one of his disciples: 'Lord, show us the Father and we ask no more', he answered: 'Anyone who has seen me has seen the Father.'[13] The context implies that the Son is *all that is to be seen of God* from the standpoint of space–time.

A hint in the same direction may be gathered from Jesus' claim that 'no one comes to the Father except by me'.[14] This might seem to suggest that only those who lived after

---

[10] Acts 2: 23 (RSV).

[11] Colossians 1: 15 (NEB).

[12] Hebrews 1: 3 (NEB).

[13] John 14: 8, 9 (NEB). Paul also speaks of 'the revelation of the glory of God in the face of Jesus Christ' (2 Corinthians 4: 6 (NEB)).

[14] John 14: 6 (NEB).

his day could come to know God; but since Jesus himself spoke of Abraham, David, and others long dead as friends of God, he must mean something else. What he seems to be telling us is that if anyone at *any* time has come to know God, then it is *he*, God-in-Christ, whom he has come to know,[15] 'Before Abraham was, I am.' Coming to know him is not just coming to know someone who can describe or introduce us to God: it is coming to know God-as-knowable-by-us: 'The Father is God. The Son is God. . . . Yet these are not (two) Gods but One.' Mysterious though they still are, there is no logical basis for dismissing such statements as incoherent or self-contradictory.

What is said in the Bible about the Holy Spirit is even more deeply mysterious, and it would be outside my purpose—and my competence—to pursue it here. Suffice it to say that Jesus himself gives a hint that there is some 'mutual exclusiveness' between human situations involving the Son and those involving the Spirit. 'If I do not go, your Advocate will not come, whereas if I go, I will send him to you.'[16] It is clear that the Spirit is *his* Spirit, but also that encounter with the Spirit is encounter with another face of God, personal[17] yet logically distinct from the Person of God-in-Christ. Once again, whatever our difficulties in plumbing the depths revealed by such teachings, there can be no justification for dismissing them as inconsistent. They show all the signs of being intended as complementary projections, to be integrated in and through our experience of applying them in the different situations to which they are respectively relevant.

---

[15] See, for example, his stormy dialogue with the Pharisees in John 8: 56-8.
[16] John 16: 7 (NEB).
[17] 'Do not grieve the Holy Spirit of God', Ephesians 4: 30.

4. *Prayer in a Scientific Age*

So far we have been asking a purely theological question: how the doctrine of God as the extra-temporal Creator of our space–time can be compatible with a doctrine of God as *knowable*. The biblical reply seems to be that to conceive of God as just *a* person is inadequate. As our Creator he has dimensions of being beyond our reach; but he has taken the initiative to make himself an accessible Agent in our created world in two personal 'projections', as God-the-Son and God-the-Holy-Spirit.

But this in turn may seem to raise a scientific problem. In a world where for most of the time the created succession of events follows reliable and indeed predictable patterns, what room is there for talk of dialogue with God? How is it supposed to work? Can it be rational, for example, to offer *requests* to God, as distinct from praise and contemplation? The objection might be anticipated that to ask God for something could make sense only if we expect him to break with scientific precedent on our behalf; and even assuming that he could, we might feel such prayer to be presumptuous and improper. We might even argue that if it is his will, we shall get it anyway, whether we pray or not. Another view, favoured for example by W. G. Pollard,[18] would accept that God can respond in Providence to our expressions of need, but only to the extent permitted by the uncertainties that limit scientific prediction.

I indicated in the first lecture (p. 8) some reasons for doubting whether either of these responses does justice to what biblical Christianity means by our *createdness*. The temptation is always to think of our environment as a created thing, but ourselves as essentially independent

[18] W. G. Pollard, *Chance and Providence*, Faber, London, 1959.

settlers in it. As we saw in Lecture 1, the Bible will have none of this. We ourselves and our fellow human beings are just as much continually dependent on the divine fiat as our environment is. God's drama is one and indivisible, both in its conception and in its moment-by-moment dependence on the agency of the Creator. It follows that if a man finds himself in a situation that calls for petitionary prayer, the circumstances that move him to pray are just as much an integral part of the Creator's conception as the circumstances that lead up to whatever God brings about in response.

The important thing to notice is that in all of this analysis so far, the standpoint presupposed is the *extra-temporal* one of God-in-eternity, and not that of ourselves as agents in *space-time*, nor even that of God-in-Christ who invites our petitions. Following our rule from the last section, we must expect the view of the situation that is valid *within* our space-time to be systematically different, without in any way conflicting with the view-from-eternity that is valid extra-temporally. Let us see, then, what difference should follow from the change of standpoint.

Imagine that you are a Christian in some desperate situation while on a mission that you believe to be God's will. Unless help comes before tomorrow, all will be lost. So you pray for help, and let us suppose that it comes in the nick of time.[19] Later on, somebody points out that unless the help had been dispatched *before* you prayed, it could not have been expected to arrive in time. Question: was it rational of you to pray for help?

The temptation here is to confuse the view-from-eternity (or alternatively the view-in-retrospect) of your

[19] For striking examples see *Hudson Taylor*, by Dr. and Mrs. Howard Taylor, Lutterworth, London, 1911.

situation with the view that was valid-from-your-stand-point at the time, and to ignore the fact that a shift of standpoint may alter the conditions that make each view valid. Without that reminder it might seem plausible to argue that from your standpoint at the time it was pointless and irrational to ask for help. With hindsight, the argument runs, it is clear that help would have arrived *even if you had not* prayed; so although your praying might have done *you* some good, it could make no difference to the outcome. If we forget that we are supposed to be discussing a *created* world, this logic may sound as nearly cast-iron as any can be; yet in fact it has a clearly demonstrable fallacy.

When we say '*this* would have happened even if *that* had not', there is always an unspoken qualification: '. . . other things being equal.' What the claim means is that if we imagine a case where *that* did not happen, but everything else was the same, then *this* would still have happened. Now when we are speaking of a created world, this qualification has a troublesome ambiguity. Do the 'other things equal' include the Creator, or only one particular drama as created? To put it otherwise, the question 'what if you had not prayed?' may mean:

(*a*) 'What if you had not prayed but the rest of the pattern of events had been the same?'; or

(*b*) 'What if God had created a world in which you had not prayed?'

In case (*a*) the answer is straightforward. In that world, if all other events had been the same and had unfolded according to the precedent we call 'natural law', the help would (by definition) have arrived whether or not you had prayed. In case (*b*), however, there is no basis whatsoever on which we can give a firm answer; for there could be no

guarantee that if God had created a drama in which you had
not prayed, he would still have made it one in which help
was sent off in time to rescue you. This is mere empty
speculation. What we do have is a firm promise that God
is 'the hearer of the prayer of the needy' and that 'in everything . . . he co-operates for good with those who love
God. . . . For God knew his own before ever they were.'[20]
Thus the rational thing for those who love God to do when
in trouble is to express their trust in this and related
promises by praying for help, confident that if their Creator
sees that good would be served by a positive response, he
will have ordered accordingly events that may otherwise
have no 'causal connection' (in the scientific sense) with
their action in praying. A Christian can indeed justly argue
that to *refuse* to ask God's help in trouble would make it
irrational for him to expect to receive it.

5. *A Secular Illustration*

It may be worth emphasizing at this stage that although
the problem we have been discussing arises in theology,
the proof that there is no conflict is purely a matter of logic.
To make this clear, and perhaps to afford a little light relief,
we might consider a parallel problem currently debated by
philosophers of science. Its classic statement is known as
Newcomb's Paradox;[21] but for our purpose we shall present
it in a somewhat modified form.

Imagine that a rich superscientist has (and has rationally

[20] Romans 8: 28, 29 (NEB).

[21] M. Gardner, 'Free Will Revisited with a Mind-Bending Prediction Paradox
by William Newcomb', *Scientific American*, **229** (1973), pp. 104-8. For opposite
views, see R. Nozick, *Newcomb's Problem and Two Principles of Choice*, in
N. Rescher (ed.), *Essays in Honour of Karl G. Hempel*, D. Reidel, Dordrecht,
1970, pp. 114-46, and M. Bar-Hillel and A. Margalit, 'Newcomb's Paradox
Revisited', *Brit. J. for Phil. of Science*, **23** (1972), pp. 295-304.

convinced you that he has) complete power to predict the future of the universe, including your future actions. He visits you one day and tells you that he has just mailed to you a sealed envelope, whose contents he determined according to a procedure he will now explain. 'I want to give you the pleasure of finding me trustworthy', he says, 'and I would like to make you a gift. Would you care to ask me for £10,000? I have of course predicted your response. I did so yesterday. If my prediction showed that you would reject my offer, I put nothing in the envelope I sent you. If it showed that you would ask for £10,000, then the £10,000 is in the envelope on its way to you now. Finally, just to show my good will and to test your trust in me, here is a further cheque for £1,000. If you wish to ask me for £10,000, you must hand back the £1,000 now. Otherwise you may keep it. Now please choose.'

Assuming that you want as much money as possible, what is the rational choice for you to make? Opinions in the philosophical journals are divided. One side argues that if you have indubitable evidence of the superscientist's predictive powers, you have no rational grounds for expecting the envelope when it arrives to contain £10,000 unless you have asked for it (and therefore had been duly predicted as doing so). Hence if you decline to ask you can expect at most to gain £1,000, whereas if you ask you can rationally expect £10,000. The other side would object that since the sealed envelope is already on its way, its contents (call them x) cannot be physically affected by what you do now, and you will gain £$(x+1,000)$ if you decline to ask, as against only £x if you ask. Ergo, whatever the contents of the envelope, you will be £1,000 better off if you decline to ask.

I confess that I take the first position; and I think that

the fallacy in the second position is exactly parallel to that which we spotted in the theological case (though the two cases, of course, differ in important respects). Let it be granted that the contents of the envelope, x, will be *physically* unaffected by your later choice. This does nothing to dispose of the datum we were given at the outset, that the value of x is *logically* determined by what the super-scientist predicts, which in turn is logically determined by (because guaranteed identical with) whether or not you ask. Hence if you choose to keep the £1,000, x is by defini-tion zero, and your total gain is £1,000. If you choose to ask for £10,000 and return the £1,000, x is by definition £10,000, which is what you gain.

If anyone protests that because it is too late to affect the contents *physically*, it would be irrational to hope to affect their specification, I would reply that this misconceives the invitation. What you were told was that *whatever* your decision, you would find that it had been correctly pre-dicted; the contents of the sealed envelope would simply be evidence of this fact. You are not invited to *affect* (in the sense of causally change) the contents of the envelope, any more than you are invited to affect (in the same sense) the prediction, already made, that determined those contents. You are invited simply to make up your mind—with the assurance that in so doing you will be *fulfilling* that pre-diction, and so can count on the promised outcome. To put it otherwise, you have been assured that the way you make up your mind, *whichever it be*, will confirm the pre-diction. So, since the value of x is logically equivalent to that prediction, it is entirely rational for you to consider what you would like x to be, and then make up your mind and ask accordingly.

Assuming that the predictor keeps his word, the outcome

(arrival of £10,000) will vindicate your rationality in choosing to ask. Conversely, those who decline to ask will find their hopes of gaining £10,000 systematically disappointed. If we imagine our superscientist making his offer regularly to all comers these must eventually fall, according to their response, into two groups, one of which will be ten times better off (per head) than the other. We must surely hope that at least after a long enough run of this kind, the 'non-askers' would come to doubt the rationality of their policy. If they did they might try to justify changing their minds on the ground that their experience had now provided them with new inductive evidence; but this would be a feeble excuse, since the 'new' evidence is only what they could have rationally predicted if they had thought clearly enough in the first place!

Finally, it may be worth pointing out that Newcomb's Paradox shows well how important it can be to distinguish logical *standpoints*. If the superscientist has predicted that you will ask for the £10,000, and has sent it on its way to you, then he knows that if *he* were in your place (but knowing what he does), his rational course would be to keep the £1,000 and wait for the envelope to add £10,000 to it. What should be equally clear to him, however, is that this would not be the rational course for *you*; for since you are the predictee, the specification of the contents of the envelope (x) is not logically independent of your mental processes. Instead, as we saw, what *you* are correct to believe is that x is defined logically by what you decide to do. The situation is a *relativistic* one, in the sense that there is no single completely definitive specification of the situation that you and he would both be correct to accept (and mistaken to reject) until after the event. It would be irrational (because incoherent) for you to wish you knew all that he knows; for one of the important things he knows is *that you do not know* the value of x. Moreover, the value of x depends on your predicted decision (still in your future); so if your desire in wishing you knew the value of x is to gain £11,000 by keeping the £1,000, this too is an irrational hope. From your standpoint, no such definitive knowledge exists to be gained, since for you to gain it would upset the condition on which it could be trusted.

As with physical Relativity Theory, this 'logical relativity'[22] has nothing arbitrary about it. It does not mean that you are entitled to believe what you like about your situation, regardless of what the other may believe. Instead, there is a strict and objectively definable relation between the two views of affairs that you and the superscientist are respectively correct to take. The point is simply that these two views must necessarily differ if both are to be correct from their respective standpoints.

The parallel between all this and the case of petitionary prayer is of course strictly limited. In the first place, a Creator is not like a predictor, whose knowledge comes by extrapolating the present into the future on the basis of precedent. For its Creator, all of the created time-dimension is equally *present*. Secondly, and more deeply mysterious still, we have reminded ourselves that the biblical Creator is claimed to have projected himself into his created space-time; not as a predictive manipulator but as one who participates in genuine dialogue with men.

But these and other necessary qualifications do nothing

[22] D. M. MacKay, *Freedom of Action in a Mechanistic Universe* (Eddington Lecture), Cambridge University Press, London and New York, 1967. Reprinted in *Good Readings in Psychology* (M. S. Gazzaniga and E. P. Lovejoy, eds.), Prentice Hall, Englewood Cliffs, N.J., 1971, pp. 121–38. Also *The Clockwork Image: A Christian Perspective on Science*, Inter-Varsity Press, 1974, especially ch. 8 and Appendix.

to weaken the logical point made by the example. It shows that there is no inconsistency between recognizing an event as an answer to prayer and recognizing that it was predictable by others—even if the prediction could have been validly made by them (though not by you) before the prayer was offered. In the case of the £10,000, it might have seemed entirely logical after the event to argue that because the money must have been on its way before you asked for it, therefore it would have come whether you had asked or not; but on second thoughts this clearly does not follow. A world in which you had not asked for it would have been by definition a world in which the superscientist would not have made the prediction that led him to mail you the £10,000.

By the same logic, a world in which you had not prayed for help would have been a *different creation*, in which there is no rational guarantee that the Creator would have given being to the train of events that met your need.

6. *The Spectre of the Inevitable*

At this point I can imagine someone objecting that in discovering the rationality of prayer we have uncovered a still knottier problem. If my praying is as much 'according to the determinate counsel' of the Creator as the circumstances that answer my prayer, am I not reduced to a mere puppet, acting out a part written for me but not generated or approved by me? Is not my whole future inevitable?

These questions express a confusion which is understandable enough, but which must be eliminated if we are to grasp what biblical theism is saying here. The distinction we have to keep in mind is a threefold one, between (*a*) a *puppet*, (*b*) a *play-actor*, and (*c*) an *agent*.

(*a*) A *puppet* is not a conscious individual at all, but a mere physical representation of motions like those of an agent, generated either by inanimate machinery or by a conscious human string-puller.

(*b*) A *play-actor* is a conscious individual whose purpose is to simulate the actions, thoughts, and purposes of *another* individual. The actor himself may or may not have similar thoughts and purposes to those he simulates. (For example, he may happen to act the part of a character who rages at views which the actor himself may abhor or admire.) But, in any case, while he is acting we recognize his behaviour as representing the behaviour of someone other than himself at that moment.

(*c*) An *agent* is a conscious individual whose behaviour is (sometimes at least) shaped by and in pursuit of his *own* thoughts and purposes. Since play-acting is one form of conscious agency, play-actors are also agents, whereas puppets are neither; and there are other forms of agency which are not play-acting.

Now whatever is meant by the biblical doctrine of divine sovereignty, it clearly does not imply that we are either puppets or mere play-actors in the above sense. The Bible is thoroughly commonsensical in maintaining that we are accountable for actions consciously taken in pursuit of our desires, good or bad. Its writers recognize, even in the most 'predestinarian' contexts,[23] that our decisions may both *affect* the future course of events and *effect* our own purposes. No interpretation of divine sovereignty that denied these things could pretend to be biblical.

The biblical position is that we are not puppets or play-actors but *created agents*. As agents, we stand accountable for our conscious decisions. As created, we live and move

[23] See, for example, the conjunction of the two aspects in Peter's attribution of responsibility to those who killed Jesus. Acts 2: 23.

and have our being by virtue of the divine upholding power. Thus no act or thought of ours could have being, apart from God's *creative* will—his 'Let there be . . .'; yet it is woefully open to us to flout his *normative* will—his 'Thou shalt . . .'. The concept of God's creative will is defined for an extra-temporal standpoint, from which our whole story is one eternal spatio-temporal fact. The concept of God's normative will is defined for a standpoint within our space-time, from which, as I have shown elsewhere,[24] our future is indeterminate in the sense that it can have no completely determinate specification with an unconditional claim to our assent (i.e. such that we would be correct if we believed it and in error if we did not) until after the event.

Thus we would quite mistake the image of creation if we took it to suggest that we are only *actors* enacting a created play for which a complete script exists already. In terms of that metaphor we are not the *actors* but the *characters*. For the created characters (in their created space-time) the future is not an inevitable fact but a spreading fan of options which they have to narrow down to a definite outcome by making up their minds. We are not doomed to enact parts that merely simulate the free and responsible agency of others. We *ourselves* are the free and responsible agents, for it is as such that our Creator has conceived us and gives us being. It would be as irrational to deny this on the grounds that our career is a determinate fact from the extratemporal standpoint of our Creator, as it would be to do so on the grounds that our career will be a determinate fact from the retrospective standpoint of some future historian.

But, someone may say, if the biblical Creator not only knows that we will pray for help at a certain time, but

[24] See p. 59 n. 22.

brings it about that we do, does this not make puppets of us? This objection once again loses sight of a vital distinction. To *create a world-history in which* you pray for help is one thing: to *make* you pray for help would mean something fundamentally different. The first refers to the creative extra-temporal work of God-in-eternity, who holds you in being as a free agent. The second would mean action *within* space-time *upon* you as an agent, either forcing or constraining you to pray. In the first relationship, God-in-eternity is not answerable to anyone in created space-time, and (*a fortiori*) certainly not answerable for what you freely do. He is just as much the Holder-in-being of wicked agents who abuse their created status to flout his normative will.[25] As such he obviously in no sense *makes them* act wickedly,[26] though he does hold in being the world-history in which they do so, and in that sense 'brings it about' that they do. So it would be a philosophical blunder to hold him *responsible* for their actions (as the manipulator of a puppet would be for its actions), even though he *gives being* to them.

In the second relationship we are at grips with God-in-space-time. In this personal projection of himself into our world as an Agent, the Holy Spirit, he is frequently spoken of in the Bible as 'inspiring' us to desire what we ought to ask for and to live better than we otherwise could;[27] but this is still something quite different from 'forcing'. If in this relationship he does at some point constrain us to pray, it will not be as a manipulator who reduces us to puppets, but as the Master and Helper whom we willingly serve. 'I will run in the way of thy commandments when thou enlargest my understanding', says the Psalmist, '. . . Incline my heart to thy testimonies, and not to gain!'[28] Or as Paul

---

[25] See, for example, Romans 9: 17; Proverbs 16: 4. [26] James 1: 13.
[27] See, for examples, Romans 8, *passim*. [28] Psalm 119: 32, 36 (RSV).

puts it, 'The Spirit helps us in our weakness; for we do not know how to pray as we ought, but the Spirit himself intercedes for us.'[29]

Nothing in the biblical doctrine of prayer teaches that there is anything *inevitable-for-us* either in our praying or in the events that come as God's answer. Even if these things were predictable-by-non-participants (as in some cases they well might be), this would not reduce our awesome accountability for the way we use the privilege of asking.

7. *Contact with God*

It is time to sum up what all this means in practice. We live in an age when scientifically based expectations reign supreme. We rightly view with suspicion claims that these should be set aside in matters of religion. Part of my purpose in these lectures has been to show that when the Bible talks of a God who acts in our world, makes himself known to us, and responds to our prayers, it does not imply that these actions necessarily break with scientific precedent.

A deistic God whose creation was a self-running machine might have to wrench the works of his machine for this purpose; but the God of biblical theism is continually active in upholding the drama of his universe, and can interact with his creatures through law-like as well as unprecedented turns of events.

In connection with petitionary prayer, in particular, we have found no basis for the suggestion that the daily Christian life of dialogue between God and man must involve continual miraculous breaches of natural precedent. Our conclusion has been that although nothing in natural science makes it in the least incredible that the biblical

[29] Romans 8: 26 (RSV).

Creator-God should depart from his normal precedent whenever he sees fit, the Bible offers no grounds for insisting that answers to our requests would have to take this form. Instead, the biblical doctrine of Providence sees our expression of need, and God's answer in the pattern of created events, as matching ingredients in the divine drama, each of which may well have normal causal antecedents in a scientific sense.

From the biblical standpoint, the petitioner's prayer is not a matter of pulling invisible causal strings to bring about a desired answer. This is what chiefly distinguishes it from pagan superstition, where the deity (or the lucky charm, or whatever) is envisaged as a source of intangible *forces* acting *within* the world by invisible causal connections that overpower the 'forces of nature'. Christian petitionary prayer is rather 'an offering up of our desires to God for things agreeable to his Will'.[30] Nor is there any suggestion that if only the right talisman is used, the outcome will always be what we desire. Instead, as we have seen,[31] our assurance is only that in all things God works for the spiritual welfare of those who love him, and that where our petitions are according to his will they will surely be heard.[32]

By the same token, there need be nothing scientifically queer about what biblical writers describe as God's dealings in Providence with those who love him. The events of daily life through which Christians grow in knowledge of God gain their special status not from any intrinsic oddity, but from the way in which they fit into the pattern of the Christian's ongoing relationship with their Giver. Read in

[30] *Shorter Catechism*, Answer 98.
[31] See p. 55 n. 20.
[32] 1 John 5: 14.

this context, the flux of experience bears from time to time a communicative significance that would otherwise be missed.

It has sometimes been suggested that a life of humble and expectant dependence on God such as the Bible depicts would destroy self-reliance and be unworthy of 'men come of age'. To this a twofold response can be made. Firstly, if our situation is in sober reality as the Bible depicts it, then to live life in any other spirit would be simply unrealistic, no matter how 'advanced in age' we may think we are. Secondly, for biblical theism trust in God is not an *alternative* to self-reliance (in the sense of the fullest development and application of one's own God-given resources). It is rather a spur to it; for only the man who has made full use of his talents has any biblical encouragement to expect God to work together with him for good. 'Work out your own salvation', says Paul, 'with fear and trembling; for God is at work in you, both to will and to work for his good pleasure.'[33]

This point is beautifully expressed by W. G. Pollard towards the close of the book to which I referred earlier (p. 52). As I was a little critical of his argument then, perhaps it may be appropriate in this connection to give him the last word.[34]

He who shares in the reality of the Judaeo-Christian insight into history as an expression of the providence of God acting both in judgment and in redemption . . . knows that the service of his Lord does not involve any denial or curtailment of his freedom. . . . Providence does not bind you and lead you about on its apron strings. Rather it comes forth to meet you, as you to it. . . . Life in a world which is consciously apprehended as

---

[33] Philippians 2: 12–13 (RSV).
[34] Pollard, loc. cit., pp. 179–80.

the expression of the will of its Creator is not a sequence of baleful incidents thwarting human purposes, but a meaningful and joyous adventure. . . . To be sure, he who knows providence can no longer sustain the proud autonomy which strives to master history. But he is not thereby cast down and trodden under foot by an overwhelming and alien power. Quite the contrary. Rather does he find himself liberated from the unrelenting demands of the isolated autonomous self, and freed at last to go forth and meet life in ever-ripening fulfilment.